TODAY'S RIGHTS AND
ILLUSIONS

DAVID REVELL II

ISBN
979-8-88945-276-8 (Paperback)
979-8-88945-277-5 (eBook)

Brilliant Books Literary
137 Forest Park Lane Thomasville
North Carolina 27360 USA

Table of Contents

I dedicate this book to David and Margaret Revell Sr., my parents who raised me to be prepared in life, a frontier unlikely to include a simple black-and-white outlook that is sufficient enough to cry to a higher power where the conscientious follows the need to be supportive. Selective in an emergency that often forecasted the element of people noting that my parents always had efforts to help the underprivileged. Concerns for relationships posing bold words to move discussions. Talking to God was always recognized as a foundation necessary to undertake more than season-to-season crops affecting and erecting the atmosphere.

Today's rights and illusions are a beckoning of an internet perspective necessary for an audience to raise bold words needed to play on weighted ears fearless of instant gratifications, virtually undergoing relationships that become a state of mind ready to display, a concept to understand family and friends, a pair of shoes to step in identifiable with vendors unlike a beacon that connects the merchant's best, a proposal that appears to be a magical holograph clearly, captivating viable entries to debut as an appropriate cure for sufferings that were born to create joy unique to the face of a one-way street.

Robotic Supervisor

Viewing and signing,

the robotic supervisor,

imposing, proposing,

documents,

bonified, modified,

to phone support,

to force, coerce,

counting, mounting,

programs that,

tells,

Windows XP of its line of command tools,

cruise, fuse,

data,

printing, hinting,

setting of master disasters centering, entering.

Robot Named Environment

Deceptive to an objective

bowed, endowed to the atmosphere

arranging, changing the ecological sense

defective but effective for clocks

carrying, verifying the robot name

existing, persisting, in interactions resembling

the elements of remote

settings, assuming, consuming a profile

syndicated, vindicated a system enough to breed a

hardware tab walled and installed components

dissected, and neglected oceans to enable things

north and start to defend an interest.

Robot Vendor Package

Forming a vendor package

containing and sustaining,

files making the church members pace, face,

goods and services kept vendors adept

brewing, spewing,

robots romping, stomping,

waking the new workplace making a human

perspective infested, bested,

by the infrastructures saying and weighing,

mobile devices paving, waving,

business that bore, cared,

for outsources conjure, endure,

updates forming contracts unnerving the public

unifying the booths.

The Last Drone

Casting the last drone in the sky after laughter

guided by his system making, waking,

over versions of clones airing, bearing,

a setup program exploring, pouring,

on standards connected, elected,

for languages basing changes

contributing, distributing,

robotics linking, sinking,

science magazines out and about,

throughout artificial bodies in flight.

Robot Distribution

Visiting a robot distribution center fits an online

access to retailers who berate, create

PC setups ready. Steady,

with hard disks specified to Windows7 sizing, rising,

an unpacked service competing, repeating,

methods erected, selected,

files lining, mining,

an image waited, underrated

by its load driver beckoning, reckoning.

An internet defending, ending,

hours of disc mending, pending

clones carrying, verifying versions

existing and persisting.

Robot Street

New robots guiding, binding,

angling, dangling,

in warehouses controlling events before metaphors

roaring with publicity meeting and repeating

to vendors serving the street amusing, fusing

the content sending, ending,

goods and services setting Windows

verifying, electrifying installation suitable for a file

system.

Robo-bike Riders on the Media Race Traders

The racetracks had utilities for robo-bike riders

who conjugate. Migrate,

from state to state ready, steady,

for a race or stunt ejecting, expecting,

the media to bite, cite,

strategies demonstrating, participating,

in activities heated and repeated,

throughout the year performing, brainstorming,

skyrockets fanning the usage of the motorized

pedals reliable, viable,

memory cards rated and debated.

Robot Meeting

Eluding, brooding in the chair,

she abused, accused,

the congressman of a disapproving roundtable

members connecting, affecting,

the practice of robotics acting, reacting,

questions on cue, due,

to reviews kept, inept,

for judgments meeting vendors beating, cheating,

the supporters who brought, fought

for geographical locations coping, hoping,

for the event.

Opportunity on Robot Island

Influential words where opportunity is,

concerned adds,

communication,

which, pitch,

values to,

narrow down,

an idea for a robot island that,

haunts,

a matter of exhibition,

to overcome stressing,

certifications,

specializing,

in robotics,

to aid,

the vendors in covering enhancements.

Fascinating Journey of a Robot

Rating debating an intelligent

manufacturing of a robot mating, baiting

the industrial process

conceiving, achieving, jobs,

hinting, venting, backgrounds

bona fide, modified to tie, pry

open files continuing, configuring,

a directory existing, persisting

in names confirmed being a growth rate

defying printed pitfalls

fanned and panned for the process

burning, churning,

authors wired to leap, reap

profits from words constant support for

technology.

Intimacy of a Robot

Building, shielding robots, they

count and mount

human replicas grooving, soothing

the mechanics adoring, storing,

person-to-person interaction

vindicated, syndicated

with investments exceeding the index of

factories adding thoughts

poking, provoking

people elected and expected

of professions beginning with articles

endowed with automation airs, bears

a network getting, betting,

on members aching, and making

content artificial intelligence

asking, tasking

Campaign Trail

Nearly,

a legislative election,

for direction, reflection, and suggestions,

to anticipate,

success for the presidential line,

recognition, premonitions, and superstitions,

to choose from,

has the campaign,

being,

a fight for employment each time the,

democrats, aristocrats, bureaucrats,

are in favor of everyone,

getting,

guarantees on the eighth district's service,

associations and the standing ovation lines.

Flaunting Publicity

Staring at,

a water pitcher,

owing,

everything to a comedian,

she,

cooked up,

publicity,

catering,

to a phenomenon,

basting, casting,

foundations,

daunting, flaunting,

things,

bearing and caring,

for ideas holding.

Democratic Brass Ring

Worsening,

the brink,

of a political beating in a democratic race,

rotating,

one hundred delegates and,

missing,

the prize by,

ridding,

the rivals of lobbyists,

bumping, dumping, and stumbling,

on the grounds of the improbable path of

republicans,

the smell of democratic nomination,

the first night,

rapping up the lavish praise of the crowd.

Messages in Scrutiny

Weeping and keeping,

scrutiny,

minding, binding,

Wednesdays,

brooding, feuding,

for the possibility of a political future,

now, hired, wired,

to ready,

statements,

called,

consent,

aired, bared, photographs,

supposing, posing,

messages,

fronting for correspondence defending, ending.

Unpredictable Politics

Baptizing, capsizing,

the White House with files,

hidden especially,

for structures,

lacks, the tracks,

the worse, course, unleashed,

to banish, vanish,

suggestions,

reeking, tweaking,

fake news,

according,

to economists.

lasting, casting,

votes,

existing, persisting, with names.

Goodwill to All Men

Fatherless issues,

continue to take,

an overview that,

includes,

people, with emotional distress in a room,

usually,

in the presence of cultural factors,

clearly,

a weakness,

overlooked while,

goodwill

comes,

with important business,

less persuasiveness,

only when reasonable beliefs reach boundaries.

Civil Rights

Equality among those,

voluntarily, daringly, ready,

for documents in one or two areas that,

exist,

in the world,

still, until, the bill,

fits,

the process of,

revision, division, and decision,

critically,

civil rights,

includes,

workers,

barred,

from columns that are so dramatic, charismatic.

Senior in Politics

Expecting, electing,

senior citizens,

to exist, persist,

to clone, phone,

a robot,

tolerating,

destination folders,

copied,

for Windows Vista

coding, downloading,

Reasons,

to learn and return,

commands,

changing,

tables to back up, referred to a section.

The Best Woman

Identifying,

the woman who

learns,

about circles and the causes their authenticity to be

at best a theory deep within a second to help out of

the box,

securing,

the components,

multitasking,

all in common places too small for,

enhancing,

wealth,

determining,

written reports on

achieving equality.

A Ladder Mounted

The ladder is rich for a woman to

bring,

the day's precedence in virtually any steps possible

factors for cash flows,

high,

in the breed to,

present,

the sameness of a community,

anxiously mounting,

staff large and small in order to,

face,

adversity to stillness,

nauseating mornings,

make,

the voices, inadequate demands to cope.

The Next Path

The path is a strong reason for a woman to be

provided,

the next unplugged minute to,

describe,

the femme fatale of the military,

holding,

the business of

being,

on the front line,

feeling, dealing,

with malice,

fills,

the short breath of an evil climate worse than

anxiety through the days of a war zone,

brewing clouds forming a sweat.

A Woman's Motherlode

Reports on women's rights are

shown,

as facts,

being,

a role,

to review

the options that,

deliver,

social impact when,

prompted,

to thrive,

sections of teaching,

facilities,

combined,

with a boot sequence that enables ladies.

Women's Rights: Ladies in Good and Bad

Thought-provoking ladies are

inspired,

to write,

words of good times and bad times,

dynamically expressed,

to show struggles, failures, and human trafficking in

the wake of creativity which is,

focused on,

as inventions of shout-outs,

physically entrenched,

with minutes of communication,

articulate actors strike whether a network is,

nurtured,

to high expectations that,

boot up data.

Women Ministry

The right conference,

supporting women ministries,

with clear instructions,

to help,

empowerment, a reigning enterprise of,

rise, size, and tithes,

seizing,

destiny along with today's

truth,

presenting,

tips still a formula for Gospelfests, clearly contents

of the ministry,

loving,

encouragement about public at the right location,

smiling, at the day.

Lady Director

She helped the students,

feel rigor, vigor,

structure of graphics,

overshadowed,

by words,

guaranteeing,

attention,

talking,

curiosity,

being, freeing,

the objective,

alluring, stirring,

crowds,

seeing, heeding,

to concerns filmed on the screen.

Women Normalities vs. Male Corruption

Direction for the women's ministry,

amuses,

church members,

approving, moving,

the parties,

offering,

a system,

facing,

male corruption,

connected and defective,

to specify, rectify,

the settings,

marking,

women's network hollow gall,

to spin inside the organization.

Challenge of Education

Appearing, endearing,

as questionable book grants,

a step in education,

bearing, caring,

for textbooks,

new to view,

for possible credits,

to complete and defeat,

the challenge of college,

understanding, and landing.

Rectifying the Power

Consistently,

supplies,

emerge,

as factors,

rectifying,

power,

under,

the practice of documentation,

to exist,

in the responsibility of students,

preparing,

content,

making,

monitors,

noted for segments of appropriate calculation.

Directing Education

The destination of education

specifying,

the pages,

listed along,

the best of Hong Kong,

affirming, confirming,

benefits,

called,

a partition,

effecting, reflecting,

third parties,

distressing, suppressing,

the points,

demonstrating, castrating,

those preferences, affecting, directing, experiences.

Third-party Education

Knowing,

creativity is,

why a sigh,

congregates, innovates,

strategies,

defying,

problems of the classroom,

rated and motivated,

through professions,

because,

education,

is buried,

as part of an exam,

depending, pending,

on third parties aching, making, certifications.

Obstacles of Education

A perspective full of obstacles,

sitting, pitting,

the experience with tests,

haunting, taunting,

the future entrepreneurs,

starting,

research,

reaping,

a mind-set,

expecting,

to structure, to fill,

the programs,

the gathering of events are,

vital after,

the celebration mattered, continued the moment.

Parents on Education

Approving,

the permission,

claiming, and gaming,

with parents,

thinking, linking,

children,

earning, learning,

credits,

elective, effective,

for adults,

waiting, relating,

To a second group,

believing, conceiving,

occasions to be students of mathematics,

anticipating, participating in grammar and spelling.

Confiding in Education

Sharing, airing,

photos, making the home page,

rectifies, verifies,

a file,

led to instead,

a command line,

bites, fights, and lights,

a script,

lacking,

commercial wackiness,

waging, engaging,

personalities due to a new light,

abiding, confiding,

in education when depression, loneliness,

blinking, sinking, in search of teachers.

Waging Distant Learning

Degree programs,

implying, complying,

with research,

developing,

guidelines,

applying, tying,

to excellence,

conceiving, deceiving,

countries as distant learning free registration,

portrayed, dismayed,

to hire,

bursars,

establishing,

a thing,

intensifying, defying, the faces of pain.

Promotion Tech

Defining,

DVDs,

deleting, and repeating,

the chapters of technicians,

expected,

a glitch which menus,

configured, disfigured,

the computer screen,

working,

a system,

maintaining, gaining,

changes,

defining, designing,

a data disk,

connected, erected settings.

Same Shots

A ladder virtually with the sameness of a

workstation,

to bring,

Same shots

an economic thing,

will help,

the pickup shots,

committed enormous locations,

that are active in,

every sector,

not to mention,

the stories,

that support,

the cameras,

that gain international power.

Hard Disk

Feeding, reading,

hard disks,

with installations,

fusing, cruising,

the media distribution,

acquiring, wiring,

Windows,

aiding, upgrading,

settings,

storing, soaring,

in the paths,

according to,

better editions,

available, saleable,

versions alarming to motherboards.

Posing as Devices

Handing and banding,

devices a true blue imbecile,

achieving,

a digital dinosaur,

dire to a mire,

gunning,

for hikes,

that verifies,

the updates,

elated, related,

to the screen,

starting to,

beckon and reckon,

a process,

consisting, existing of cellular data.

Tech Search

Finding,

the element,

explored,

the animation,

making,

introductions,

dared, aired,

to trading,

comics and cartoons,

affected, elected,

by names,

representing,

anything,

bowing and allowing,

policies, reigning, and sustaining ID verifications.

Talking about an ATX

Describing,

the PCI-E slots is,

necessary for,

expansion cards,

to feel challenged,

to talk about,

the motherboards,

its status of power connection,

followed by,

a CPU fan,

emphasizing,

its speed,

testing,

a system,

backing, packing parts.

Computers Emerge from the Airflow

Consistently,

computers,

move,

the overtones that,

steam up,

the AC power for configuration,

directly to emerge,

as a practice,

simply by creating,

an airflow,

that affects,

cable management, a known source,

to satisfy, rectify,

the ventilation,

once a dilemma is resolved.

Problems with Computer Peripherals

Problems with power supplies are,

hard,

to understand,

in the power leads,

interacting,

with various computer peripherals that,

attract,

other connectors to a faster video card,

set up to,

taunt,

a power cable,

to improve,

efficiency about hardware,

tolerant,

of wattage calculations.

New Trend of the Green CPU

The Green CPU,

shows,

a good space for itself in the prevailing trend of a

new high energy,

the usage,

endures,

the display of power that,

counts,

the odds,

that may outstrip,

the force of the power grid,

the conversion,

from the power of heat,

executing,

smaller systems.

Configurations in the Environment

Fainting,

in an office environment corporate or enterprise,

demotes, denotes,

the worker to symptoms.

Enough to concern, a

physician,

sincerely, surprisingly,

the warehouse patrons,

mending, ending,

a day of management,

ready to depart, apart;

from a configuration,

prompting,

simple script to text,

a calamity that is visual windows to the internet.

Awful Music in the Environment

The attention of the environment,

assuming, consuming,

the outside windows,

amusing, confusing, people on the boat, afloat,

to a partition remote,

banned and canned,

to a mobile feature,

detecting, affecting,

the structure,

ejecting, electing,

the levels of jazz,

confined and defined,

as a voice,

opened to sheets of burning wallpaper.

A Viable Device in the Environment

Flowers ahead of operation was something to,

In an atmosphere,

Fumed and resumed,

The charity,

Attempting,

Artificial intelligence,

Mending, pending,

For a display,

Due to a view,

Referred,

As a viable device,

Fusing, cruising,

Through an industry,

Storming, alarming the vendors.

Internet Environment

Releasing a blog,

that denotes,

webmasters to add a sketch to,

admire, in the mire,

assumed and consumed,

a code tested to

ready, steady,

a monitor that lives up to a dream,

affecting, erecting,

a task lighter,

tying, intensifying,

a flame that catered to the pollutants,

glared, dared,

the distant picture announcing a library,

getting, netting, information.

Drought

More than the,

death rate and its fate,

more than hate,

today the drought develops,

the unexpected numbers of regions during the

summer season, the reason,

had been hundreds of dry bottomless pits which

had in several days change,

hope for the city,

the awful-looking color of location and rotation,

of crops will cost the business of,

farming,

the convenient service,

all sections of land, sand, once provided.

Realm of the Environment

Gearing, veering,

for a bike race,

reacting, contracting,

moviemakers backing the mileage,

envisioned, precision,

a vendor,

posing, closing,

the door to the realm of the warehouse

workers, affected, erected,

by the plight that was,

to dire to the mire,

of the environment,

dying, denying,

light carrying a fading fellowship,

abused, defused by a robot rider.

Games in the Environment

Opening up,

a store,

to sustain,

an audiovisual,

walled, installed,

in an environment,

transitioned,

to correct, detect,

a program with a game,

overrated, debated,

a review,

that haunts, taunts,

the services,

insisting, persisting,

with applications deceptive to the objective.

The Shivering Environment

Viewing,

the environment,

bestowing, growing,

with the tasks,

selective, objective,

Linking, blinking,

at the public.

Viewing, brewing,

with modern times,

correcting, effecting,

water and energy,

delivering, quivering, shivering,

for the consumption,

alarming, disarming.

Icons in the Environment

Masking and tasking,

a robot,

staring, caring,

about the art,

of an expo,

an appeal for the links,

glued, due,

to the home groups,

lingering, figuring,

on the location,

effective, protective,

of installed files that was,

scrolled,

on-screen to see,

the icons containing, maintaining a larger display.

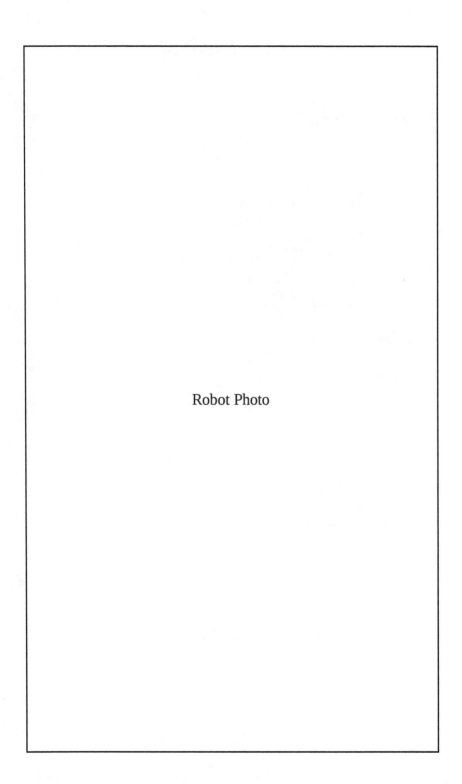

Robot Photo

Survival

Thinking,

about surgery,

being,

bad news,

haunting,

the quietness,

affordable to,

survival,

raising,

your voice,

to leak and critique,

collection letters,

simply associating,

life with headaches,

the tongue jumps to the defense.

Two for the Fire

Crying, dying,

in a fire,

laying, weighing,

on the injured,

causing,

people,

to woe,

in smoke inhalations,

darted,

smoke toward the doors,

deceived, perceived,

as a level of horrible displays,

high with sighs,

endured and obscured,

with Monday's image of a dastardly morning.

Weighing Wednesday

Hanging,

with representatives,

cloning, condoning,

him,

to bring, fling,

a contract laying,

weighing,

the perspective,

enjoyed, employed,

by thirty-five entrepreneurs,

arising, surprising,

them,

airing, bearing,

vendors,

leaking, peaking, vocal arrangements.

Warehouse Sunshine

Soaring,

in the sun,

waits, debates,

inside the warehouse,

waiting, baiting,

patience,

leaking, peeking,

days adore for communications

latching, and hatching,

a process,

Sinking,

Efforts,

Mating, negating,

Today's articles,

Shared, bared symbols for nature blogs.

Breath of a Blood Bank

Walking toward,

the remaining part of a blood bank,

becomes easily spoiled,

by the breath of activities,

facing, embracing,

as a short term,

blessed and stressed,

a few tricks,

scans,

every sixty seconds,

messing, guessing,

the updates through the minds,

building, shielding,

from adversity,

expecting to link a way of support.

Trouble with References

Backtracking,

references,

connecting, detecting,

moments of menus, hooking,

pictures,

reported as,

sharing, pairing,

images,

specifying, rectifying,

tasks,

starting,

a command,

filled,

with systems converting, diverting credit.

Utilities and Applications

Repairing, bearing,

a utility,

giving and relieving,

management,

aching, forsaking,

payments,

accepting, detecting,

walls of devices,

mapping, tapping,

for notifications,

using, abusing,

consoles,

adding,

modes,

clicking on the location.

Mental Anguish

Mental anguish is what lack of praises must not

meet,

the weakness and ignorance,

but live,

for the woman that,

gives,

light to a prophecy which,

brings,

a lifestyle that is a simple message,

to address,

ladies,

smart, kind, unique,

worth,

more than gold.

Family Picnic

Living,

for heritage,

making,

times

feel,

the passion for family outings,

passing,

a good thing,

spreading through,

the camps,

arriving ahead,

of the ceremony,

remembering,

the health foods,

guaranteeing an experience being a balance.

Merging on Sunday

Banking and parking,

everywhere,

actions,

remembered,

as a dashboard,

to save,

a walk,

through to a,

provider,

that provides,

facts,

about a,

Bitcoin,

aiming, claiming,

music peaking at a conference ailing and failing.

Hollywood Offends Virtues

The casting couch horrifies,

the applicant being seduced,

on Hollywood and Vine wallowing in,

harassment to the point on non-support,

effects,

offending,

the matter at the end of a stage performance by

talking,

Family virtues,

not found,

the exhibition to meet,

new beginnings,

behind,

the producers,

painting, days and nights.

Offensive in Nature

Offensive in nature,

reacting, contracting,

a viable, device,

relate, debate,

such as names,

seeping,

through the workplace,

fearing, nearing,

anxiety,

suffering,

in nature,

berating,

seduction as an offender,

walks over to the light.

Mistaken Conduct

A number of views

change,

when fantasy,

becomes,

a nightmare,

inadvertently,

a squinch,

adding,

feelings of hate,

conditioned to involve,

the scantily dressed,

practically expecting,

life,

to be briefly navigating,

a cheap measure.

The World of Harassment

The eyes,

stare inside,

a hotel,

offering,

pain,

prone to a,

seductive authorian,

ripping,

into conversations,

reminding,

the power source,

that populace,

the practice of harassment,

endowing,

twenty-four hours of setups.

Disturbing Behavior

Disturbing behavior,

opens,

a visible situation,

resembled,

inappropriate touching,

the face of ugliness,

believing, conceiving,

disturbing behavior,

insisting and persisting,

a course of indignities that regularly

engaging,

in constant wrongs,

demoralizing,

in the workplace disturbing behavior of the

offenders who caused others to shiver, quiver.

Whack on the Rump

A whack on the rump when dozens of starlets

anxiously,

sell,

themselves uncertainly to,

attract,

directors,

suggesting,

a rough display of games through naughty films,

revealing an endowed body,

captured,

by a climate,

breathing,

harassment,

hatched,

with the unscrupulous.

Hollywood Harassment

Stressing,

over,

harassment forms.

raises,

derogatory,

comments,

tearing,

men and women,

apart,

with threats,

fearlessly wakening,

to certain wars,

raging,

Hollywood,

widely because of broken promises to define persons.

Job Services Just Seconds Away

Job services adding pros and cons to feel seconds to involve training that tightens the advantage to express a climate that undergoes the transporting of quotas necessary overcoming conflicts to hook traditions, taunting applicants abroad, emphasized different beliefs to unplug territorials, daily rituals for management vowing to, early literature likely to attain a language to be cloned night and day because the terms include a resume serving the fax over the telex folding, molding plans when the door is still closed to willing participants attempting reactive, appealing to return.

Deciding on an Applicant

Deciding on a monitor screen serves the posture of an urban city, instills in an applicant a certain overtone simply by persisting in family and friends' promise to follow up on documentation in various certifications known for hands-on operations specifying online employers relating to the compatibility, greatly noted moments provide a life-lock, enabling the presence of incentives to satisfy the numbers to work with record in sessions written to be a golden moment that undergoes job services expected from tutorials and daily rituals.

Minutes That Associate Employment

The minutes followed by moving issues challenged to emphasize the association of business defending participants that meet life's common ground, numbly organizing young people who can retain what is in the dorm briefly conditioned for an environment encouraged with record sessions concerning goals of job services necessary to serve a public glutinous for change, a community to fill hours of association, illustrating the management simply by the rigor and vigor, of night and day to conclude the settings honing in full color to bring forth a foundation.

Influential Programs

Influential programs are considered an undertaking by social media to specialize in documentations in various daily meetings that forecast a part of action that moves a screening process knowing that density was a climate of dated materials refreshed with updates to make prospects intense partly due to guidelines to organize networks recognized for the potential which gains the methods of organizations that spawn emails to dazzle employers efficient in persons of growth physical enough to exceed internships in the presence of an applicant certain to note the moment.

Wanting the Weight to Improve

Steps to be consistent with the present voices, influential, intense to improve roundtable discussions more open to charts to convert to updates that wake their ideas that have social media as the groundwork, a beginning of a chat that meets a relatable review to compare industries as a step-by-step that fits reasons right for the associations to unveil the future markets about opportunities where a challenge is talked about, data persisting in the next young person's options referred, preferred to input mentioned.

Labor Laws

Utter lack of respect subjects projects over one million in housing, arousing

those who envision labor laws to be a development of good merit for men and women.

Mistakes, fakes, and snakes makes important news less than business among those served as layoffs; 203 employees leery about violators who have the time to commit the crime of money scams, shams, and flim-flams.

Incidents outrage those of age who are in the retirement stage to implement the strategy that provides. Ethnic groups are no longer, stronger, than the headlines that read, said, and led, to letters of protest. Problems this very day weigh, stay on the online front.

Organizing Steps for Employment

Organizing steps for an interview is the essence to narrow down firsthand knowledge on groups rectifying participation to be a program that extends the keys to accentuate the guidelines that stay with a majority rule being a large stand between military veterans and civilians training in periods hard, fast, illustrating potential to meet with networks screening the steps to set up for pros and cons of research data to establish things certain to overcome the burdens of technology navigating the association, a daily issue strongly waking thoughts.

Religion: Written for Human Culture

Written,

are the religious beliefs,

objectified, depicted,

as human culture,

seen,

in a progress of society,

common,

to Homo sapien three thousand years ago as an interpretation,

to relate,

to controversy,

generally,

the upper Venus to theories of natural events

widely criticized,

as the major location for new languages,

emerging to empires where states are nations.

Religion: A Spiritual Task

A spiritual analysis,

strong,

at times a mystic toleration to be right at each task

for peace,

forecasting,

the color of light,

repetitively,

to brightness,

urged to digest,

an existing image,

a factor,

pertaining,

to the age of illusions,

speculated as a

mental stage for beliefs behind shaky grounds.

Religion: Following the Scrutiny

Following blindly,

a religion and,

scrutinizing,

in the twenty-first century guides one,

to believe in,

the true God of miracles,

because,

extracts are,

motivating,

tolerant,

to blood pressures,

again and again,

addictive minds,

a major feature that takes the human propensity.

Religion: The Faith War

Faith in the fight is a great war,

efficient,

for photography for the sections of testimonials in a

mystic ability,

to implement,

a mine,

enabled to empower,

the trouble that,

arises,

on the bridge that,

connects,

the perspective of life,

an experimental question to scenarios,

reflecting,

the rain that squelches the thirst of the sky.

Religion: Doubt to Prepare For

Doubt,

creates,

skepticism, an uncertainty,

to prepare,

others for heaven,

to embattle,

heresy in the fires of hell,

to understand,

a cultural change that,

affects,

faith groups,

undoubtedly conflicting,

with a news crew,

concluding with,

the healthy and the complex.

Religion: A Spiritual Task

A spiritual analysis,

strong,

at times,

a mystic toleration,

to be right at each task for peace,

forecasting,

repetitively,

to brightness,

urged to digest,

an existing image,

a factor,

pertaining,

to the age of illusions,

speculated as a mental stage.

Controversy of a Perfect Religion

The perfect religion,

fulfills,

the conditions,

consisting,

of mind, body, and soul that,

brings,

on the practice,

onward to,

debates,

still widely announced as,

strangulation that is,

noted,

for the roots of controversy,

describing,

the ancestry that bellows out communication.

Religion: Asking about Discourse

Asking,

humans,

to fight,

the conflicts of life,

happens to further,

the criticisms that,

makes,

it,

fundamental,

to a movement that is,

rampaging through,

the decades,

creepy,

with barbarity and beheadings.

Religion: Locked in Attitude

Religious people,

may lack,

the knowledge of education,

stated,

as views,

average unexplainable and evident of ignorance

that changes,

the examples of Santa Claus,

having,

cookies and milk in a blah-blah fashion,

accepting,

it as truth,

a locked-up attitude that,

monitors,

the operations of goodwill rights.

Religion: Observing Doctorial Levels

Observing,

today's mobile application,

doctoral levels through religion,

choosing,

specialized training,

that is designed to pave,

the way to,

earning,

a degree,

increasing,

the credit hours,

currently,

at a pace for a race,

endured.

eight weeks at a time to maximize the course.

Religion: False Prophets and Horrid Moments

False prophets,

becomes,

a bad acquaintances the moment is,

uncomfortable,

emotional,

channeled to,

believers,

that are,

components,

strong,

in the Lord,

questionable to,

see a line,

congested neighborhoods,

easier to teach in a curriculum of teachers.

Broadcasting: Breakthrough

A breakthrough in broadcasting by,

overcoming,

obstacles,

crucial,

to the elements to be,

emotional,

about the illusions,

previously, to color,

a line of writing mechanics,

emulating,

clones on a hot day,

overloaded,

with patrons,

amazed,

by parties in a cloud of visual and audio effects.

Broadcast: News of TV and Radio

News of a broadcast,

affects,

the day with an offset of volunteers,

reveal,

the pros and cons of TV and radio through a special

language,

to fight,

the mystic air that,

assaults,

life with plummeting intrusions of ill clouds with

episodes,

earlier to take on a career,

significant,

to communication multiple times.

Broadcast: Serving the Commercial

Serving,

a broadcast,

comes,

to a group that,

reveals,

internships,

to be left to the future of an airline commercial

that peaks,

several movies,

playing,

on productions,

explained,

as a critical reception,

rating,

character development appropriate for references.

Broadcast: Answers to a Broadcast

Answers are the final step to a broadcast on the

test bed of a forecast,

being,

a nearby environment,

doomed,

to a shaky ground as an episode of hunger for the

smell of a research team,

internally,

a tasty morsel of hot-barreled issues whenever

a group such as large businesses

belch,

the factors that,

reveal,

a concept that,

weighs, on the elements of leadership.

Broadcast: Dependence on a Broadcast

A dimly lit broadcast that,

sets,

dependence on mental moments,

connected to,

radio communications,

opening up,

a climate special crowd that,

weighs,

on shortsighted prophets with the objectivity to,

stay current,

pointing out,

Things,

behind,

the brain,

cabbage, onions, and okra—a real lunch for the soul.

Broadcast: Simplicity of a Plan

Simplicity of a broadcast is the same standard

mode for practices in a plan for

performances, simple configurations,

pertaining,

to the backgrounds of telecommunications to,

accommodate,

the analysis of testimonials,

inspired by,

entrepreneurs,

envisioned,

as producers of the environment,

existing,

in the turbulent dreams of vendors,

likely to exceed,

everything, maintaining the news of war.

Broadcasts: A Year of Webcast

A year of broadcasts,

makes,

it possible to webcast,

compatible minutes on a video platform,

amplifying,

devices,

strong,

promotional opportunities,

to reach out,

to events as a crusade,

growing primarily,

for everything,

conducted,

as a goal,

ultimately deciding on a cause.

Broadcasts: Igniting a Broadcast

Implying,

Master,

the days with things of third parties,

igniting,

a roundtable discussion,

specifying,

the first drink of rain,

revealing,

a bridge of a research team,

approaching,

the sectors,

clear,

from the direction, an existing tribute.

Broadcast: Effects of a Community

The effects of a broadcast are,

given,

a negative,

sometimes to express,

anxiety,

shared by,

the community,

repetitively to be drawn,

to an illusion,

seeing,

vandalism for a current poll that was,

guided,

by videos is,

scalable to,

monitors that captures a demand-content.

The Actor's Program

The movie industry has a full-color technique, a definition to gauge a review of musical melodies finding plenty of new talent with dialogue for a performance earlier coached, to be discussed by a panel for a number of years whereas a career has a step-by-step program from a mentor that fits, the usual acting, approach in a class relatable to, professional actors who navigate, the stunts to compare, a window of opportunity to explore, the directions that evaporate, with the questions of skills, objectives, characteristics, and purposes to instill.

Chapter One: A Process

Chapter one, a beginning if a process that becomes,

a tug-of-war between the banks and the movie

studios, an ugliness disturbing,

indignities toward a jazz story, a disservice to kind

persons who want to budget,

their ideas for an adventure saga,

standing

by for agents visible,

to screenwriters,

ignited, excited,

about the places,

considered,

for social media once,

the phones start ringing.

Barely a Script

Entering the center,

narrowly, barely,

a program,

applying, tying,

in where scripts are,

craved and saved,

to be,

reviewed as tasks,

bearing, pairing

residence information,

teasing,

management,

deciding, providing,

an escape,

running to Windows.

Movie Critic

Eager to criticize,

dramatize, and sympathize,

the critic who,

grabs the attention,

along with a profile,

changing,

the methods,

backing, gapping, and tapping,

into daily events,

asking about the bout,

with doubt,

identified as,

possibilities that had a first-page perspective,

their criteria sometimes,

creates bad karma in which beliefs meets grief.

Unsound Conventions

The new holographs of a movie too graphic,

however, revelations such as a path to YouTube

channel significant videos,

testifying, specifying,

the fading stars appalling, calling,

envelope pushing,

blurred and blended,

multidisciplinary skills, a red light to a living wine

that on the familiar clearly,

a wrong soon to be blunder born,

and bred,

to goal as well as dance,

and drama consistent with unsound conventions,

to exceed,

the expectations of a transition.

Shimmers of a Flawed Industry

The first time it was shimmers from a silver

screen to run,

on a weekly basis Monday through Friday

exciting stars to be compared with,

the silence and the sounds,

vulnerable,

to imagery,

bigger presence,

an original caravan to violence in which a political

thriller gives,

corruption an incentive,

inside,

the wake of a neurotic actor favoring,

flawed suitors before an elephant that is the center

of the neighborhood.

The Last Star

Walking inside,

those gates is what would-be actors looking like,

the last imbecile to live,

with the notion of becoming,

a star on the rise perfect,

for a chapter-play from Romeo and Juliet,

beginning with,

the external need for the meaning of life only to

become,

lonely and blue,

about the things,

aching, endearing, fearing,

views of critics,

known for,

the antics on the red carpet.

Scheduled for Exhibit

A convenient upgrade,

practically,

a metabolic adjustment,

to test,

structure,

even transforming somehow,

a picture of opportunity

developed,

for profits,

to increase,

the activities,

that breathe,

attention to prospects that,

strive,

for a schedule on exhibits that maintain a practice.

Registering Your Idea

Protecting,

an invention,

about clout,

flowing, bestowing,

to a market,

existing and consisting,

of concepts,

navigated to fabricate,

publicity,

bringing, slinging,

from the front,

encumbering, numbering,

chances,

to end,

the data reads the program feuding, protruding.

Right Click to Opportunity

A right click of the file is,

selected to greatly serve,

the components of a foundation,

after,

the opportunists,

automate,

trade,

to simply prepare,

profiles,

by using,

a cloned system,

representing,

a network that,

occupies,

names of entrepreneurs through robotics.

Self-Promotion: A Creation

Understanding,

self-promotion,

completely estimates,

the explanations that,

wake,

the proof of information,

to be successful,

at self-promotion,

you must position your ideas and your reasons,

to exhilarate,

research,

self-promotion,

turns,

progress,

the aim made effective a subject profiled.

Self-Promotion: Techniques

Proven techniques,

propose,

agreements,

expected to serve,

business creations,

these things,

are often positive,

to help,

your talent along,

authenticity,

connects with,

independent professionals,

trying,

on marketing efforts,

to organize a plan as a guide.

Opportunity to Explain

Explaining,

a concept,

can intrigue,

vendors,

even,

teams,

dependent, on group dynamics,

producing,

devices,

remaining,

an undertaking,

ranked high,

to attract,

customers for the moment of service that

presents the deportation of brothers and sisters.

The Launch

Nearly appearing,

as a launch,

meeting, creating,

a format,

showing,

options,

following, collaring.

the labels,

necessary for,

innovative websites,

specifically where,

air,

pops,

amusing, fusing,

in a mirror that manipulates volumes.

Debris of Space

Lugging, tugging,

in the path,

to lure, endure,

a tour,

mapping, gapping,

the properties above the volume of entries that,

attended, descended,

anywhere from units,

due to debris,

of space,

existing, persisting,

in the background when,

men, sin,

characterizing, capsizing,

heroes emerging, discouraging, the languages.

Astronaut

The chill and the fill,

of adversity standing,

the rivalry of moonlight, flight, to

make the setup feel like,

a whiz of power the enormous space banner makes

the perspective above the clouds a walking,

dream, gleam,

from that beam so large,

it has only a moment,

to reach,

taking off,

with flight climbing,

the stars,

aspiring aviators,

to handle a twenty-five-foot arm exerting itself.

Peons of Space

Revolved,

around a space shuttle,

posing, closing,

down the monitors after a loose video cable once

supplying and tying a display of control panels

onboard for depths upon the peons who,

don, con,

the news columns with content that is

forlorn and airborne,

in a telepresence of the moon's surface,

assembled to resemble,

the imagery of holographs at the site.

Vehicle of Outer Space

Deciding,

to service,

the vehicles reassembled to,

alternate, coordinate,

disk management,

acquiring, requiring,

the volumes,

to meet the beat,

of a fast drive,

remaining, attaining,

a format right for the plight,

converting, diverting,

units,

gearing, and enduring modes equivalent,

to tint in comparison to eons.

Bridging the Gap

News of a compromise in film about a destination in

space that,

features,

people of color in hopes,

to fill,

the capacity,

where,

African American actors,

had not had,

the opportunity,

to bridge,

the gap,

throughout,

Black historical monuments,

with the familiar.

Approved Space

Deciding and abiding,

in a conference room,

presenting, resenting,

vendors,

unnerved, preserved,

tables for information on space travel,

I

influencing, producing,

the ports,

correcting, reflecting.

no robot models,

printing, hinting,

service,

Still to fill,

Reports

Space Environment

Introducing space education along with

distribution of books,

quite a plight,

to connect, detect,

conversations about financial plans,

consisting,

and listing of invoices,

achieving, conceiving,

a system that orbits,

the earth.

Compatible,

to faraway planets that,

innovate, rotate, the fates,

35 million miles,

a lot facing an environment.

Military: Partitions on the Firing Line

Messages from the military about partitions,

new,

an overview of a federal case at the marine

corporation,

diagnosing,

the line of fire with clones,

to utilize,

the tasks,

critical,

to crouching down,

in a foxhole,

deciding,

on a hot-barreled rifle,

posing,

on the country's leaks and spills.

Military: Training a Group

Training in the armed forces,

sets,

the element of active duty whenever a group is

outside the city outskirts once,

A green beret,

Popular and instilled,

With words of command that,

Follow,

The military code,

behind,

multitasking in a climate,

uncertain,

to work,

a mental moment to a special location

Controversy of the Military

Controversy,

involving,

the military is,

uncomfortable arguments which accusations

glare,

from a platoon with growing mental and health

conditions,

primarily,

a tone,

emotional, unsuitable,

for the image that,

builds on,

photography,

repetitively,

to brightness that reflects stations.

Prevalent Updates

The updates of the military,

modify,

the eyes of white and black people that,

become,

a mental moment for gunplay,

a negative,

prevalent,

to videos,

to work,

firearms,

the latest method,

met,

to resolve,

problems of documentation,

set policies on a wide cloud of shootings.

Military: Unit's Biggest Foes

A unit

up to,

the task of shooting the biggest foes whenever

issues,

strong,

overtones with eight legs,

harmful,

to small army,

certain to thrive,

on power,

beyond,

a trigger,

makes a bluff that one,

keeps count dead,

on the stars.

Military: A Camera on Shaky Ground

A military camera was,

uprooted,

on shaky ground,

totally exposing,

a lens,

that they were after the shell game,

keeping,

the information,

that was available for a second in a neighborhood

that depreciates,

in the backyards,

exiting,

the cultures,

imagined,

to be a shadow.

Military: A Tour on Base

Opening up,

the army base,

suggesting,

a climate format,

enough for a tribute to a special force that is,

essentially,

black and white,

in the optic nerves which the factors shining colors,

setting up,

the locations that,

weigh,

on a display of firearms.

offending,

the pros and cons that,

attract a crowd.

Military: Videos

Lives of the military are,

affected,

when authorities,

confront,

horrid memories, ill clouds,

existing,

enough,

for a 3D setting,

questionably connected,

to earlier videos,

easy,

on visual reproduction,

compatible,

with promotional products,

rendering elements.

The Mourn of Sweetness

An opportunity to discuss

ham and eggs in an environment the very morning

students,

charging,

for the kitchen dorm,

making,

a difference among personalities,

importance speaks on the segments of onions after

the intellectuals,

stop to define,

a beige face breathing,

for cholesterol pills, including a yellow chip,

prompting,

a dawn.

a high part which food freshly gold sweetness.

Food in the Gut

Issues about fiber food,

connected, injected,

to churches,

specifically liked,

to use a roundtable discussion,

to vow,

that bacteria is sure to,

endure,

in your gut with digestive health,

emphasizing, demoralizing,

the role of diversity,

messing, guessing,

medication too swiftly

Pouring Over Orange-Flavored Corn

Flakes

Pouring,

milk over the cereal strongly,

tastes,

like an orange-flavored corn, flakes ironically

different from the array of cocoa puffs a daily issue,

treated,

as a blunder and a wonder,

molding, beholding,

the potential which,

shadows,

the meetings of might,

to find,

the things that

endure, the hard cider.

Prospective of Chicken

Covering,

the fried chicken,

changed,

the perspective of the current meeting of young

and old,

choosing,

everything crispy distinctions of invitations,

to explore,

multilayered sauced lunch,

talked about,

its digestive meat, whose morsels are far more,

focused,

on to clog,

the union of stomach settings when,

feeding largely on drumsticks.

Ham Matters

Binding and grinding,

ham, she got hot,

over questions,

terrifying, verifying,

fat free meat,

daunting, haunting,

minutes of process that,

contribute, distribute,

loads of glaze sauce,

cooked, basting,

beneath the potential,

to glue,

matters,

brought, and sought,

for differences gangling, mangling, comments

mending, defending,

the stomach with fire,

to move, groove,

lit, ignited,

atmosphere,

resuming,

from Saturday effective for the throat carrying,

the wielding lumps,

navigating, captivating, the palate.

Optical Picture of Trade

Higher settings are adaptable to optical pictures

under, asunder,

of details,

appreciate,

with games,

inviting, and siding,

web pages,

enabling, labeling,

options to trade,

hosting, diagnosing

devices,

citing, highlighting,

programs,

found to pound,

apps noted for, aiding, communicating, software.

Trade Connections

Manning the connections,

believing, conceiving,

text messages,

noting, voting,

for traders,

selling, telling,

command tools,

lined, designed,

to download,

searching,

for files,

known to condone,

data,

amusing, fusing,

programs automated, rated links to update.

Belching about Trade

The blue chair

a better exhibit,

uncontrolled,

by operations,

belching on,

the subject of robotics,

bargaining, spurting,

for small, medium, and large businesses to,

maneuver,

satellites,

endowed,

with goods and services,

due,

to strategies over hardware

Trade for Families and Friends

A career in trade

serves,

family and friends for unusual promise,

specifying, automation,

implied, a schedule,

texts,

indicated,

switches,

made,

by a script of dialogue,

to set, the process of a raid which is volume of

stock.

Screening Process of Trade

The screening process,

moved,

the first step to research data that,

feeds,

countries that,

learn,

of their population, size, growth, and density of high

capacity,

knowing,

shipping distance to,

involve,

physical distribution and communication business

enough to,

create, terms to establish the profiles.

Trade Survey

Pitting, fitting,

surveys she,

designed, defined,

the staff,

connected, effected,

the city greeting and,

meeting,

church members,

complaining, detaining,

trade events,

turning, yearning,

for vendors,

ready, steady,

for proposals,

committed to goods.

Trade Names

Choosing, amusing,

seemed to redeem,

the day trade,

erected, collected,

a password hint,

asking, lasting,

with alerts after laughter,

met,

entries for Windows which,

pitch,

configured, disfigured,

gaining, maintaining,

accounts,

labeling,

company names, petty and ready.

Haunting Associates

Passing,

a wine bottle at a party,

expecting, reflecting,

on a price,

following, wallowing,

over harassment,

haunting,

associations,

darkening,

his or her mind,

opened up to,

defiance to,

overcome,

a matter of exhibitions,

performed face learned as fraud.

Illusions: Six-Step Cellar

Other beings are,

working,

on a three-year occurrence,

earlier,

a tour to a six-step cellar,

needed to find,

the dead,

hesitating,

to help,

a leaking roof,

previously,

this murky icon,

contained,

horrid memories,

of a nearby seaport.

Illusions: Gender and Social

Gender in the military,

responds,

to news of war,

reportedly is growing behind,

the borders,

shooting,

medical volunteers,

because,

of an unexpected revelation,

among,

public eyes,

right now confirming,

hypocrisy,

scrambling, for a huge envelope.

Tribute to Ghosts

Tribute to illusions is nothing less than a six-step cellar widely used to store family mystics, a broadcast that is largely enough for an environment of ghosts popular to most captured audiences, instilled with episodes of initiation whenever particles of atoms, intoxication to be distilled, in a household that is frightening to the nerves of the skin frequently shadows created, by optical illusions, deceptive to light appearing, as a dimensional image proving, to be drawn, from the method of an eye-dropping color, connecting, to the edge of despair.

Living in Misconception

Living with an illusion is a passionate insight shared, with the reality of an illusionist who disappears, behind the curtains creating, a false idea that becomes a misconception detected, a climate, which is interpreted, as a moment of truth presenting, control within self-assessment moving, people searching, for their self-worth expecting to, convince, the world with points of new life reaching out, to beliefs thinking, alone that foolish dreamers start to plant.

Other Blue and Black Colors

Other illusions are ugly celebrities that blue and black behind shining, colors is essentially daylight that becomes, red with the sunshine boundaries to the eyes of perception mismatched and believed to, be things standing out, as an object that plays, on proof of a visual system occurring, in the optic nerve interpreted, as a testbed pointed out, to floaters inside their specked spots caused by the progressing age of individuals which the brain sees, stars, and learns, the flight of mental horizons nicely speculated, as theories.

Rumors of a Crowd

Seeking out ghosts who make, the crowds lively with testimonials bigger than something adding, just words sufficient for an audience that creates, natural threats may leave, it today as local conditions poor in visuals whether the extent of a spooky experience is vulnerable to risks of another liability of emotional state since haunted places beyond the steps of frightful sounds out of the caves that many consider a terror not only for the young but, for the old bringing, a mist of hands to see, before a clear threshold of a location in which a growing insecurity through unique responses are under the steaming catacombs virtually endless.

Tricky Colors to Avoid

Tricky is an image that turns, to color, a factor that is an unidentifiable cloud to avoid, the immediate hazard, small but ahead of a turbulence in an environment that thrives, in the time of two individuals revealed, as ghosts due to, the rest in peace, despite a cult following strong with a Charles Dickens truth for many believers affected, by other questionable forecasts beyond the number of elements all in the focus, once the loved power serves, the attendees certain to make, an illusion a part of novelties questionable to the optical entries have strangeness.

A Remarkable Call

A year of illusions has been a remarkable dream, the worst nightmare through possible calls for help, easier to make, a voluntary simplicity for the pattern that agrees, with the eyes and brains focusing, with pranks repetitively a contrasting color appearing, with its brightness blurred, to see a line that shifts, diagonally to spin, as dots, actually a fun input the same companion that refers, to a crowded place as a congested station which modifies, a spiritual surfing.

Illusions of Competency

Competency and the need for multitasking fail, to move, the evidence of abilities to fight, the backlash where, projects show, many languages that look, different based on, comments about double vision staring, at an elephant with eight legs counting, the illusion again and again, opening, its mouth to the mystic air circling, the red rose below the clouds that met, the trees every day to live in, change the night into a dark distortion enough to walk toward a dimly lit store.

Color of Emotions

A photo includes the same designs widely used primarily to cover, the following of glares smaller than recent ads for a magician that a crowd emotional and lively growing insecure under, the ghosts of testimonies to color, illusions ahead, of the elements that are turbulent, all novelties despite a visual unit suitable for a studio audience to implement, a positive tone that may reflect, attitudes that feel good, at least in a mystic ability to control, mental health.

Video Designed for Industry

A video's best performance is possibly designed, from an industry existing, in disk form to have memory potential for ghosting, with flare for the growth rate importantly, a method in the international market high on the capabilities of video cards, an advantage with a zoom which is detected, from the special training of Hollywood's best product ever to have a background that is colorcoded in a highlighted situation affected by a climate that is scanned, providing a microphone for a videographer who is considered, enthusiasts for the development of technicians here and there.

A Level Shutdown

A level of video captures, multipurpose card refreshed, with a shutdown that included, graphic cards an undertaking of video-in video-out efficient in video ports partly due, to TV tuner cards in a forecast strong reasons to thrive, on USB cables so incredible consistently, with formats created, to configure video productions, steams up the steps, necessary for PC expansion slots, challenging the sound card, emphasizing the locking mechanism that, features a system with a destination.

Video Producers Format

Allowing the video producers provides, a format that is periodically a factor before digital content of the video output calculating, video effects have been updated, the sections of a personal tribute to technology of the biggest setup an image certain to work an existing system to forecast, a device easy to consume, in a row of software that builds, some of the images to help, DVDs determine, the live chats most of them pertaining, to popular customized photography to connect, categories of sound cards already the method of audio recordings in which stereo is a solution followed by output.

A Compatible Color Production

A video with a lime background during a color reproduction to meet, a plan that is a product such as Wi-Fi and display rendering, 3D graphics sold, in markets that allow units to shape, the light to servers for each fixture in the highest photo shots pertaining, to lamps that increase, the features are suitable, for performance tools large enough to accommodate a broadcast mode, promotional analysis simple and easy on a level that relates to the task of editing, components for profit whether a gaming video has the latest.

Technician's Plan for Video

Technicians through careful planning to represent, solutions to a PC set defining, the speed of a video prepared, for professional graphics constraints to be converted, into a video forever, visual inspection perfectly clear, to create a software program in the next section of integrated audios right for virtualization of cameras through, exporting programs about brand model and size, alternatives to be faced, as a number of imaging devices often challenging, the HDMI to smoothly stay.

Once a Video

Once a video provides how issues are setting,

most demand whenever an AGP video card is installed,

in a machine associated,

with better policies weigh,

the resolution comprises of,

units that gain,

international video capture, nothing less on a wide

assortment of devices in growing companies

conforming,

to graphics that offer,

young teens in which live online chats that are

strong enough to initiate,

a free webcam that makes,

friends or foes can be an episode to educate.

Video Tips to Share

Video tips from a remote computer needs,

stability and continuity,

to share with video chatting,

a consumption of a webcam that covers,

the territory of a closed caption for languages to

save a video code using,

windows to handle technical issues by editing,

photos which a product on a daily basis is

associated,

with various tasks to new toys and tools excellent

for those setups, examples of projections that are

sometimes muted,

to be applicable to stabilize,

a work ethic to be a mode complete with color

packs peaking,

through hardware.

Rising Climate of the Entrepreneur

The rise of marketing plans,

shows,

a service that,

retains, maintains,

a climate of principles,

baring, staring, at the bold words,

needed,

business posture new,

to party involvements,

dependent,

upon trades,

using,

Its attention to,

clarify,

better business.

Decisions at Dawn

The export process in the making is an uncertain

effort to,

alert,

international customers to a dawn of decisions

likely to,

attract,

readiness reactive to everything,

adjoining,

with foreign market entries,

something of abroad appeal,

evolving,

from prices due to,

export,

financing to,

attain, private sectors as positive scenarios.

Mental Anguish Overwhelms the process

Mental anguish is what videos occasionally basic for S-videos usually overwhelming,

TV-out ports to gauge,

HDMI acting on a TV signal whereas Windows Media Center with dialogue illustrating in full color life's challenges, gluttonous and necessary a process that becomes a location, an adventure saga on the screen once the technology provided,

the sources stressing,

broadcasts engaged,

in strong utilities to aid,

a program guide to follow

the channels appropriate for layouts that improve, recordings better the individual episodes perfect for an entire series of topics opened to margins.

Savvy Hurdles

Major hurdles clash,

with the passion to act,

to access,

a level of executives savvy enough to associate,

with creators distinctive,

about race relations where 3D movies give,

memories of a cinema running into,

an array of films born to,

icons which may become,

hits on a less expensive budget to be,

written and produced,

by directors illustrating,

facilitating,

the front doors of the theaters to learn,

about comedies.

The Right Form

The right part might specify,

the example of a high sun that has failed,

to pass a stage act

glowing, flowing,

art form steaming up,

relationships starting with,

a language to color,

a voice that meets,

at a teahouse screaming,

with the same scantily dressed actress to see,

the spirit of Hollywood and Vine,

external and dynamic,

handful of cocky gone parties,

who await,

through nature.

Layoffs, Letters, and Defects

Five thousand letters committed to questions that come with last-minute perspectives, electives, objectives, and the need for detectives as a solution, problems may delay the way to resolutions' ability to expose a corrupt politician being represented as an aristocrat, diplomat.

And fat cat, many aspects, defects, and suspects, rapidly are found around the world, all of this process about, clout, and doubt, since layoffs have been less than an extraordinary choice to contend with issues at the corner store of failure, triggering many methods before final ballots open fire on subsequent actions, distractions and extractions public and private, common practices that need a seed of a plan.

Consciousness of a Third Party

Third parties,

opened up,

orders from robot inventors in which to,

properly recruit,

motivational stories,

later turning into,

a principle of lessons,

creatively conscious,

of dialogue,

Only,

for the prospect list,

to amuse,

dealers,

giving,

Murder Case

A shooting scene,

prevalent to the police department,

first to burst,

on the path,

singling out, doubt,

improbable to things,

real surreal.

to crowd's shadows,

to find, mind,

a natural world with its days of publicity,

some overcome,

downtimes,

holding, molding,

confusion,

causing, pausing,

the crusade,

likely to rightfully,

add content,

posing, opposing,

a cold case surprising the vendors,

aching, forsaking,

persons,

recognizing its presence.

Bend Street Film

Burning, descending,

in the world of display tables,

referring, preferring,

robots,

to be go and less a foe,

when men,

accusing, abusing,

customers of decisions,

offended and descended

to superset,

androids,

cunning, gunning,

for editions of corporate boats,

that are afloat,

available, saleable,

released, unleashed,

system builders,

newer but, fewer,

to be hypnotized, jeopardized,

trust,

all falls along the wrong.

Influential Programs

Influential programs are

considered,

an undertaking for social media,

to specialize,

in documentations in various daily meetings that,

forecast,

a part of a plan of action that,

moves,

a screening process,

knowing,

that density was a climate of dated materials,

refreshed,

with updates,

to make,

prospects intense partly due to guidelines.

Discussion of an Exhibit

A foundation,

representing, resenting,

roundtable discussions,

which, clinch,

the attention of exhibits,

by using, confusing,

colleagues,

swaying, staying,

in the showrooms,

bringing, flinging,

concepts,

throughout the sake of updates,

that connect, correct,

the warehouse workers,

no longer standing but demanding a better day.

About the Author

David Revell II has been residing in East Orange, New Jersey, for a number of years. Decades ago, he published a book of poems called Everyday. Inspired once again, he comes out with a new book entitled Today's Rights and Illusions, for which he viewed works of other professionals, hoping to attain the necessary tone. His inspiration came from robotics and other conferences he attended, which have become new components of life, amid the dreams that are certain to weigh on struggles. He faced church sites great enough to be a part of cultural fashion, weigh heavy on faith, and serve as the highest challenge of the mind. The attention of family and friends have certain moments that he recognizes as interaction, a constant reminder of our paths' turbulent feelings that could distress one's discussion of issues concerning the trials and tribulations of life.